LIVING
IN THE
Promises
of God

By Tamara Okma

Living in the Promises of God
Trilogy Christian Publishers
A Wholly Owned Subsidiary of Trinity Broadcasting Network
2442 Michelle Drive
Tustin, CA 92780

Scripture quotations marked NIV are taken from the Holy Bible, New International Version®, NIV®. Copyright © 1973, 1978, 1984, 2011 by Biblica, Inc.™ Used by permission of Zondervan. All rights reserved worldwide. www.zondervan.com. The "NIV" and "New International Version" are trademarks registered in the United States Patent and Trademark Office by Biblica, Inc.™ Scripture quotations marked NKJV are taken from the New King James Version®. Copyright © 1982 by Thomas Nelson. Use by permission. All rights reserved. Scripture quotations marked TLB are taken from The Living Bible copyright © 1971. Used by permission of Tyndale House Publishers, a Division of Tyndale House Ministries, Carol Stream, Illinois 60188. All rights reserved Scripture quotations marked TPT are from The Passion Translation®. Copyright © 2017, 2018, 2020 by Passion & Fire Ministries, Inc. Used by permission. All rights reserved. ThePassionTranslation.com.

10 9 8 7 6 5 4 3 2 1
Library of Congress Cataloging-in-Publication Data is available.
ISBN 978-1-68556-177-2
E-ISBN 978-1-68556-178-9

Dedication

You are holding this book in your hands because my family, friends, and clients believed and encouraged me when I did not believe in myself. I sincerely thank each one for the love and support you provided to me in the process of writing these pages. God is so good and never gives up on showing all that He has for those who love Him. Thank you, Jesus, for this journey that we have been on together. I am so thankful for all that You have shown me through Your Word!

Table of Contents

Prologue

Have you ever thought to yourself, "There has to be more to this life. Am I missing something?" I want to take you on a journey to show you that there are secret treasures hidden, promise after promise, for the children of God in His Word. As I have grown in my relationship with Jesus, I have begun to understand that there is much, much more. I would read something, and it would feel like it leapt off the page. What I began to see was beyond my wildest dreams. God began to show me promise after promise for those that would receive His Son Jesus and be in relationship with Him. As I would read these verses, I began to realize that we did not have to prove ourselves, work harder, strive or anything else. The promises were already yes and amen for those that are in Christ and who would believe Him (1 Corinthians 1:20). What Jesus did on the cross through His death, burial, and resurrection has given us access to these great and precious promises.

In my life, I tried to be a good Christian. I thought I had to earn God's love. I really did not have a foundation of what I already had. I hope, with what took me over twenty-five years to learn, that I will be able to simply begin to share the amazing promises of God. He loves you so much and has given His very best, His Son Jesus. I now have a new destiny because I realize how God sees me, which I learned through His Word. As I would receive what God was showing me, I would see more and more promises. Honestly, I was overwhelmed with the magnitude of what belongs to the children of God. It was too good to be true, I thought. I must be missing something. It took a while for it to finally become real, but God never gave up on me. He just showed me more and more. Through this book, I will show you how much God loves you. How your identity changes when you receive Jesus as your Lord and promises that belong to the righteous (that's you, if you have made Jesus the Lord of your life). This is just the beginning of the promises that belong to God's kids. So, pull up a chair and get a warm drink. Get ready to receive from God and begin to understand that there is much more in this life. The promises of God are a gift for His kids and are just waiting to be opened. Enjoy!

Tamara L. Okma

Living in the Promises of God

Introduction

We are about to enter into the beautiful Word of God. Through the years, I have found many verses that talk about promises. "Those of us that have received Jesus as our Lord and Savior, all the promises are yes and amen" (2 Corinthians 1:20). I want to begin this journey of living in the promises of God by showing you verses that speak about them. This is just the beginning; I believe that there are over 7,000 promises for the children of God that are found in His Word. Wrap your mind around that! If there are so many promises, then why are we, the children of God, not walking in them? The promises are for anyone who will grab hold and believe in them.

I have learned a few secrets from the many years of being on this journey with God. The first step is to get the Word of God inside of you. Spending time in the Word and getting to know Him is key. I have found many Christians not really getting to know God until something happens in their lives, then they beg God to do something. God wants you to realize what is yours ahead of time in His Word. This is why it is imperative to sow the Word into your heart so that it will give you strength and direction when needed. The more seed you plant, the more harvest you will have. The more you know and believe, the more your life will start to line up with what God says. God's intention is to have us get to know Him through His Word, so that He will be able to walk and talk with us through our daily lives.

The second secret is to speak the Word. Faith comes by hearing and hearing by the Word of God. The more you hear yourself speaking the Word, your faith will begin to be renewed. There have been times that I would have to say, over and over again, who I was in Christ. I honestly can say that I fought God with the calling that He put on my life. I thought it was impossible for me to become what He was putting deep down in my heart. I had to overcome doubt, fear, worthiness, my upbringing, etc. It took many years of going over and over what God said about me versus how I saw myself. Renewing your mind in what God says takes time. But in the long run, you will be so grateful that you invested the time. For those who are just starting out and beginning this journey, I hope that I can help by sharing with you the beautiful verses that I have found over the years. No matter where you are or where you have been, God wants you to grab hold of His promises.

The third secret is—to persevere even when you do not see the manifestation of the Word of God right away. This does not mean it is not working. You must believe and receive it no matter what your circumstances say. For example, when a farmer sows a seed in the ground, it does not reproduce a harvest right away. It takes time, good soil, patience, watering, etc. to reap a harvest. This is the same as sowing the Word of God in your heart. As you sow, it will take time, patience, watering, and the good soil of your heart for the Word to grow. For many years, I had the knowledge of the Word in my head. I believed it, but I still doubted it at times. I knew what the Word said, but most of the people around me did not believe the way I did. When I was younger, I remember having childlike faith. I was healed miraculously from a car accident at the age of three and a half. I pulled away from my sisters' hands and ran out into the street. I was hit in the head and then dragged under the car. To make a long story short, the doctors did not give my parents a lot of hope. People who did not even know me began to pray for my healing. A local church heard about the accident and surrounded my parents and family. It is because of the powerful prayers of those people that I am here today. Because of this healing, I just believed in God and His truth. The problem was, as I got older, most people around me did not believe that way. It was a fight for me to continue to stand on what I believed. Through the years, my faith was tested again and again. It was through the hard times that I would go to God and His Word. It was the only thing that would give me a sense of hope. I had to learn to stand on what God was showing me. I did this by renewing and speaking the Word of God. A cool thing happened, I have come to believe what God says is mine. Satan has been stealing from me and

I have had enough (John 10:10). I am going back after the years (generations) that have been lost. God gave me these verses many years ago found in Joel 2:25a, 26 (NKJV):

> "So I will restore to you the years that the swarming locust hath eaten, You shall eat in plenty and be satisfied, and praise the name of the Lord your God, Who has dealt wondrously with you; and my people shall never be put to shame."

> "As for you also, because of the blood covenant, I will set your prisoners free from the waterless pit. Return to the stronghold, you prisoners of hope. Even today I declare that I will restore double to you."

Zechariah 9:11-12 (NKJV)

During this time of my life, my family that I grew up in was a mess. My parents' marriage was very unstable. We always seemed to go from one crisis to the next. I felt like I was always walking on eggshells. Then I read these verses, and something inside of me said that these words were for me. I grabbed hold of that Word, and I got it deep in my heart. At this time of my life, I did not understand what I am telling you. I was in the beginning stages of learning about the Word. I really did not have anyone teaching me. My mom was learning herself. She would try to pass on to me what she was discovering. I listened at first, but after a while, I would tell her to stop preaching at me! When we are young, some of us think we know everything. I was no different. All you moms and dads know what I am talking about. Back to my third secret, sometimes we will not see the manifestation of God's Word right away.

"Now faith is the substance of things hoped for, the evidence of things not seen."

Hebrews 11:1 (NKJV)

At times, we will have to stand in faith even when we don't see it. I have been standing on some promises from God for many years. I have not seen the full manifestation yet, but I know in my heart I will because of what it says in His Word. My job is to stand in faith on what the Word of God promises.

"Your kingdom is an everlasting kingdom, and your dominion endures through all generations. The Lord is trustworthy in all He promises; and faithful in all He does."

Psalm 145:13 (NIV)

"Who made heaven and earth, the sea, and all that is in them; Who keeps truth forever."

Psalm 146:6 (NKJV)

I invite you to take this journey with me in living in

the promises of God. There is so much for you to discover. I hope, through my journey, that I can share what I have learned. So, sit back and enter the beautiful Word of God. Here are some verses to get you started.

"For no matter how many promises God has made, they are Yes in Christ. And so, through Him the 'Amen' is spoken by us to the glory of God" (2 Corinthians 1:20, NIV).

"As for God, His way is perfect; The Word of the Lord is proven; He is a shield to all who trust in Him" (Psalm 18:30, NKJV).

"One man of you shall chase a thousand, for the Lord your God is He who fights for you, as He promised you. Therefore, take careful heed to yourselves, that you love the Lord your God" (Joshua 23:10-11, NKJV).

"Turn my eyes away from worthless things; preserve my life according to your Word. Fulfill your promise to your servant, so that you may be feared" (Psalm 119:37-38, NIV).

"We do not want you to become lazy, but to imitate those who through faith and patience inherit what has been promised" (Hebrews 6:12, NIV).

"Blessed be the God and Father of our Lord Jesus Christ, who has blessed us with every spiritual blessing in the heavenly places in Christ" (Ephesians 1:3, NKJV).

The Love of God

Chapter One

What do you think of when you ponder the love of God? Many of us may remember the song as a kid, "Jesus loves me this I know, for the Bible tells me so." I went through many years of believing in God, but not really understanding the depth of God's love. I knew in my head that He loved me; however, I related to Him as a distant God. I did not understand that He longed to have an intimate relationship with me. I had to renew my mind in God's truth, which I found in His Word.

I struggled seeing God as my Father. I guess this was because I did not have a close relationship with my own father. I knew my dad loved me, but he was unable to give me the love I needed. As I have grown into my adult years, I have learned that people cannot give away what they do not have. I believe that many of us are looking for this love in other people and things but have not realized that it is only found in God. We need to understand and be full of God's love, so that we can give it away to others. It is so important that we learn what God's Word says about God's love. It is the foundation of receiving everything else.

Remember, if you are born again in Jesus Christ, then you become a child of God (Romans 10:9-10). This is the first step in understanding God's love. He looks at us as His children. Let's take a look at a verse that talks about God being our Father:

> "See what great love the Father has lavished on us, that we should be called children of God! And that is what we are! The reason the world does not know us is that it did not know Him!"

1 John 3:1 (NIV)

The word "lavished" in this verse means spending or giving with liberality or abundance. It can also be characterized by lavish, profuse, extravagant giving.[1] God wants to lavish His love and blessings on you. He wants to have a relationship with you the way it was originally intended to be. Jesus was sent to redeem what was lost. Because Adam and Eve choose to disobey and eat of the tree of good and evil, they disconnected from their relationship with God the Father. They experienced a spiritual death; they lost the communion they had. When Jesus died on the cross, access to the Father was restored. Jesus said in John 14:6 (NKJV):

> "I am the way, the truth and the life. No one comes to the Father except through Me."

---

1 The American Heritage Dictionary, 2ⁿᵈ edition (Boston Massachusetts, Houghton Mifflin Company, 1985), 718.

So, when we confess that Jesus is Lord and receive what He did for us, we become the actual children of God! Here are a few more verses to show you that you are a son or daughter of God when you receive His Son:

> "'I will be a Father to you and you shall be My sons and daughters,' says the Lord Almighty."

2 Corinthians 6:18 (NKJV)

> "But as many as received Him, to them He gave the right to become children of God, to those who believe in His Name."

1 John 1:12 (NKJV)

But wait, it gets even better! If you are a child of God, then you become an heir. Everything Jesus has, you now have because you are in Him!

> "And because you are sons [and daughters], God has sent forth the Spirit of His Son into your hearts, crying out, 'Abba Father!' therefore you are no longer a slave but a son, and if a son, then an heir of God through Christ."

Galatians 4:6-7 (NKJV)

What does it mean to be an heir? 1.) A person who inherits or is entitled by law or by the terms of a will to inherit the estate of another. 2.) A person who succeeds or is in line to succeed to a hereditary rank, title, or office. 3.) One who re-

17

ceives or is expected to receive a heritage, as of ideas, from a predecessor.[2] God has so much in store for us; however, if we do not renew our minds to what the Word says about who we are, we will never walk in the fullness that God has intended for us. This is the desire of my heart to show you what God has for you. When I kept pondering the Word in my heart, my mind was being renewed and my eyes began to be opened to the truth. My life began to change when I would meditate on these verses. Let's take a look at another amazing verse that talks about God's love.

"Now hope does not disappoint, because the love of God has been poured out in our hearts by the Holy Spirit who was given to us. But God demonstrates His own love towards us, in that while we were still sinners, Christ died for us."

Romans 5:5, 8 (NKJV)

God loves you so much and wants to have an intimate relationship with you that He sent His Son Jesus to pay the price that we could not pay. A cool visual to have is when Jesus took His final breath on the cross, the thick curtain in the temple was split in half from the top to the bottom. This curtain was in front of the Holy of Holies in the temple, which represented God's presence. Only a high priest could enter one time per year. The curtain being torn in two represented that access to the Father was now available to all people.

2 The American Heritage Dictionary, 2nd edition (Boston Massachusetts, Houghton Mifflin Company, 1985), 603.

Because of Jesus, we all now have access to our Father God in heaven. Look what it says in Hebrews 6:19 (TLB),

"This certain hope of being saved is a strong and trustworthy anchor for our souls, connecting us with God Himself behind the sacred curtains of heaven."

God has given us His promises and His oath to those who take refuge in Him. When you get to know your Father God through His Son Jesus, you will have a strong and trustworthy anchor for your soul. It literally leads you into His inner sanctuary and His presence. As you spend time in His presence, you will begin to see the promises of God and what belongs to you.

"Every spiritual blessing in the heavenly realm has already been lavished upon us as a love gift from our wonderful heavenly Father, the Father of our Lord Jesus-all because He sees us wrapped into Christ. This is why we celebrate Him with all of our hearts."

Ephesians 1:3 (TPT)

The promises and blessings are already there and waiting for the children of God to make a withdrawal. Here is another way to think about this concept, Jesus has already given us everything that belongs to Him. When you receive and make Him Lord of your life, you are saved. In the Greek, the word "Sozo" means to save from material and temporal deliverance from danger, suffering, and sickness. It also means "to bring safely through, made whole, to guard, keep, and preserve."[3] This is what God wants for all people.

> "For the Son of man has come to seek and to save (sozo) that which was lost."

> **Luke 19:10 (NIV)**

Don't lose one more day! Satan is trying to keep you from this love and all the promises that are for you. John 10:10 says that Satan is the thief that comes to kill, steal, and destroy, but Jesus came to give you life and not just life, but the abundant life! The Word of God is a gold mine of secret treasures for those who keep digging into it. Psalm 119:162 (NKJV) says it this way, "I rejoice at Your Word like one who finds great treasure." The more you meditate on these verses, the more you will see how very loved by God you are.

Let's review what the Word tells us so far:

- God will be a Father to those that would receive His Son Jesus.

- He calls us His sons and daughters.

- We are now joint heirs with Jesus.

---

3 W.E. Vine, Merrill F. Unger, William White, Jr., Vine's complete Expository Dictionary (Nashville, TN: Thomas Nelson, 1996), 547-548.

- God the Father wants to lavish His love on you!

Let that truly sink into your heart. I believe many Christians do not see God this way. I know that I did not until I began to renew my mind in what the Word of God said. Even after I could see the promises of God, it took me a long time to believe them. However, the more I heard them by speaking them, the more my faith grew. It is not enough to hear God's Word once a week in church. You need to personally see it for yourself. For when you can see the Word of God, it will come alive to you if you will receive and believe it. Then your eyes will be open to all the promises and what belongs to you as a child of God. Let's continue on our journey of understanding how much God truly loves us.

Soaking in the Love of God

Chapter Two

"The Lord has appeared of old to me, saying: 'Yes, I have loved you with an everlasting love; therefore with loving kindness, I have drawn you.'"

Jeremiah 31:3 (NKJV)

Let God's love draw your heart towards Him. My sincere hope in showing you all these verses and more to come is to show you the promises that are prepared for those who will love God in return. As I have been on this journey, I have been absolutely amazed at what God has shown in His Word. I have had all these verses, but honestly felt overwhelmed by the magnitude of God's love and promises towards those who will believe Him. Here is another verse, while you read it, see yourself before Almighty God.

"The Lord your God is in your midst, the Mighty One, will save; He will rejoice over you with gladness, He will quiet you with His Love, He will rejoice over you with singing."

Zephaniah 3:17 (NKJV)

Receive this love from God. He will save and rejoice over you with gladness. He will quiet you with His love and sing over you. I believe we need to spend more time soaking in and meditating on what God says about how much He loves us. Read the scriptures over and over until it begins to penetrate your heart. Speak the verses over yourself out loud. The Bible says that faith comes by hearing, and hearing by the Word of God (Romans 10:17, NKJV). Ask yourself, what are you feeding on, the Word of God or what you hear around you? God has so much He wants to show you, and it begins with a relationship. We have a choice to receive this love from the Father. It is for anyone who will receive His Son Jesus and what He did at the cross.

> "Yet in all these things we are more than conquerors through Him who loved us. For I am persuaded that neither death nor life, nor angels nor principalities nor powers, nor things present nor things to come, nor height nor depth, nor any other created thing, shall be able to separate us from the love of God which is in Christ Jesus our Lord."

Romans 8:37-39 (NKJV)

Meditate on God's love for you. It is vital for you to start to understand this truth from the Word of God. It is the foundation of receiving everything else from Him. How can you receive if you do not know that you are loved, that you are worthy to be loved? My prayer for you is that your eyes of understanding will grow to know how much God truly loves you.

> "That Christ may dwell in your hearts through faith; that you, being rooted and grounded in love, may be able to comprehend with all the saints what is the width and length and depth and height to know the love of Christ which passes knowledge; that you may be filled with all the fullness of God. Now to Him who is able to do exceedingly abundantly above all that we ask or think according to the power that works in us, to Him be glory in the church by Christ Jesus to all generations, forever and ever. Amen."

Ephesians 3:17-21 (NKJV)

Once you start to see this, then you will start to understand who you are in Christ! Our true identity must be discovered and possessed through our relationship with our Father God. Let me show you this through my own journey. I have been asking God for the past couple of years to show me how much He loves me and how He sees me. I have struggled with seeing myself how God sees me for quite some time. This has been a long process, but when God began to show me what His Word said about me, I was then able to see myself in a different light. For example, I have been petrified to speak in front of people. I actually used to even be afraid to pray for others. God began to allow me to see myself in His heavenly courts. I would have these visions of standing in front of God, just talking with Him. I have heard in my spirit, "Tammy, come up here." I then walked up some stairs, and I sat in between Jesus and Father God. I just thought I had a great imagination and did not think much of it. Through time spent in the Word, I began to find verses that supported my visions. Here are some verses that God used to show me how He sees me.

"To the one that is victorious, I will give the right to sit with Me on My throne, just as I was victorious and sat down with My Father on His throne."

Revelation 3:21 (NIV)

"Open for me the gates where the righteous enter, and I will go in and thank the Lord. These gates lead to the presence of the Lord, and the godly enter there."

Psalm 118:19-20 (NLT)

"There's a private place reserved for the lovers of God, where they sit near Him and receive the revelation-secrets of His promises!"

Psalm 25:14 (TPT)

"He raised us up with Christ the exalted One, and we ascended with Him into the glorious perfection and authority of the heavenly realm, for we are now co-seated as one with Christ! Throughout the coming ages we will be the visible display of the infinite, limitless riches of His grace and kindness, which was showered upon us in Jesus Christ."

Ephesians 2:6-7 (TPT)

"And now, because we are united with Christ, we both have equal and direct access in the realm of the Holy Spirit to come before the Father!"

Ephesians 2:18 (TPT)

I share all these verses to show that one way that God will speak to us is through His Word. I would read and speak these scriptures over and over so that my thoughts would line up with God's thoughts. Please hear my heart: I am not smart enough to put all this together on my own. God has been revealing who He is and is looking for someone to believe Him. God even showed me what has been holding me back. Are you ready? Here it is:

"Fear and intimidation is a trap that holds you back. But when you place your confidence in the Lord, you will be seated in the high place."

Proverbs 29:25 (TPT)

I have struggled with fear and intimidation my whole life. Nothing like being direct and to the point. I come against this fear everyday by speaking 2 Timothy 1:7 (NKJV), "But God has not given us a spirit of fear, but of power and of love and of a sound mind." This is also a great verse for anyone who struggles with their thoughts, depression, or anxiety. God gave you a sound mind, in the Name of Jesus. I hope by being real with you about my own journey, you can see the beauty of God's Word. He has shown me that He sees me victorious, as an overcomer, a warrior, righteous, strong, and co-seated with Christ. This is just the beginning. There are many more verses in His Word, but you get the picture. If God sees me this way, I need to see myself this way. It has totally changed my identity. I am still a work in progress, but thank goodness I am growing! If God will do this for me, He will definitely do it for you. He is not a respecter of person.

> "He who has My commandments and keeps them, it is he who loves Me. And he who loves Me will be loved by My Father; and I will love him and manifest Myself to him."

> **John 14:21 (NKJV)**

Did you catch that? It said that Jesus would manifest Himself to us. I have said it before and I will say it again, spending time in the presence of God is never wasted time. Over the years, I had no clue what God was planting in my heart. I did not always understand what I was reading. I didn't have all the answers, but I kept searching for the truth. I did not come out of a family that was full of God's Word. Don't underestimate what God will do if you just surrender your heart to Him. I am a perfect example. I will leave you with Revelations 1:5-6 (NKJV):

> "And from Jesus Christ, the faithful witness, the first born from the dead, and the ruler over the kings of the earth. To Him who loved us and washed us from our sins in His own blood, and has made us kings and priests to His God and Father, to Him be glory and dominion forever and ever. Amen."

You are kings and priests in God's eyes! It is about time we rise up as His children and see ourselves as loved and cherished by God. We were created for intimacy with God. He wants to pour out His love to overflowing in us, so that we can then flow out to others. God wants us to be His hands and feet. However, He cannot use us until we see ourselves the way He sees us. God is not holding back on us. We are holding back on God. He sees us as conquerors, and we see ourselves defeated. He sees us healed, and we see our sickness. Make God bigger than your circumstances. Instead of making your issue, sickness, or problem bigger, tell your circumstances how big your God is! Before we can do this, we need to understand how much He loves us and is for us. Knowing God, His Word, and His promises are vital to living this life to the fullest. Let's continue our journey in seeing the promises that belong to you.

Additional Verses on the Love of God

"The Lord is compassionate and gracious, slow to anger, and abounding in love. For as high as the heavens are above the earth, so great is the love for those who fear Him; as far as the east is from the west, so far has He removed our transgressions from us" (Psalm 103:8, 11-12, NIV).

"Yet I will not forget you. See, I have inscribed you on the palms of My hands; your walls are continually before Me" (Isaiah 49:15b-16, NKJV).

"For God so loved the world that He gave His one and only Son, that whosoever believes in Him should not perish but have eternal life" (John 3:16, NIV).

"The grace of the Lord Jesus Christ, and the love of God, and the communion of the Holy Spirit be with you all, Amen" (2 Corinthians 13:14, NKJV).

"For I know the thoughts that I think towards you, says the Lord, thoughts of peace and not of evil, to give you a future and a hope" (Jeremiah 29:11, NKJV).

"The Lord has appeared of old to me, saying: 'Yes, I have loved you with an everlasting love; therefore with lovingkindness I have drawn you'" (Jeremiah 31:3, NKJV).

"The Lord your God in your midst, the Mighty One, will save; He will rejoice over you with gladness, He will quiet you with His love, he will rejoice over you with singing" (Zephaniah 3:17, NKJV).

"But God, who is rich in mercy, because of His great love with which He loved us, even when we were dead in trespasses, made us alive together with Christ and raised us up together, and made us sit together in the heavenly places with Christ Jesus, that in the ages to come He might show the exceeding riches of His grace in His kindness toward us in Christ Jesus" (Ephesians 2:4-7, NKJV).

"He who does not love does not know God, for God is love. In this the love of God was manifested toward us, that God has sent His only begotten Son into the world, that we might live through Him. In this is love, not that we loved God, but that He loved us and sent His Son to be the propitiation for our sins" (1 John 4:8-10, NKJV).

"We love Him because He first loved us" (1 John 4:19, NKJV).

Our Identity in Christ

Chapter Three

"For as he thinks in his heart, so is he" (Proverbs 23:7a, AMP). For many years, I struggled to see myself the way God saw me. I never thought that I was smart enough or good enough to be used by God. I did not grow up in a strong Christian family. Neither my mother nor father were raised in Christian homes. My grandparents, early on in their lives, were part of Christian Science, Freemason, and Eastern Star religions. This made it all the more difficult for me to know the truth. However, my parents did the best they knew how. They were both saved, but they were learning about being a Christian as they went through life. I say all of this to explain that I did not know the simple foundations of who I was in Christ. Understanding my new identity in Christ has been a life-long journey. I have learned that it is not about how I see myself or how well I can walk out this life as a Christian. It is all about Jesus. Everything He did was for you and me. We need to realize the price has already been paid and that Jesus came to restore you. Who we are in Christ is receiving what Jesus did for us at the cross.

God's intention was for man to see his identity in Jesus Christ. It is not about us being good or doing all the right things, but seeing how God sees us through His Son Jesus. We limit God and His promises in our lives because of the way we see ourselves. You cannot possess more than you think you are! How do you see yourself? The Bible is full of verses that explain who you become after giving your life to Christ. When we see ourselves in Christ and what belongs to us, it will change the destiny of our lives. Many of us, because of a lack of knowledge really do not know who we are. This is what I hope to help you see what the Word says about you!

Where is your identity? How do you see yourself? We need to see ourselves the way God sees us, in order for us to accomplish what He has for us. Our lives will never really change, and we will not live a victorious life if we don't see that we are valuable and precious in God's eyes. This goes back to understanding how much God loves you and that His greatest desire is to be in a relationship with you. As you are in relationship with Him, you will start to have a revelation of who you are in Him! Your identity in Christ is so import-ant. If you do not know who you are in Christ, you will just become what media, people, and society say about you. The truth of the matter is that insecurities come from our trying to get our value from something or someone other than God. You will reflect the very thing you are currently submitted to and this is what will shape you. Wouldn't you like to see how God sees you and submit to His ways? He created and knows you better than you know yourself!

God sees and loves you the same way that He sees and loves Jesus! When you truly understand who you are in Christ, it will change how you relate to Him. It will help you realize that your source of strength is from God and your understanding will begin to open up to the blessings God has for you. How do we receive the blessings of God? Through His Son Jesus.

"His divine power has given us everything we need for a godly life through our knowledge of Him who called us by His own glory and goodness. Through these He has given us His very great and precious promises, so that through them you may participate in the divine nature, having escaped the corruption in the world caused by evil desires."

2 Peter 1:3-4 (NIV)

How we see ourselves determines what we will receive in life (good or bad). We must understand who we are in Christ to receive what is ours! Do not be deceived and let the enemy steal from you! You are a joint heir with Jesus if you have received Him. Everything Jesus has, you have! Look what He says in John 16:13-14 (NIV):

"But when He, the Spirit of Truth comes, He will guide you into all truth. He will not speak on His own; He will speak only what He hears, and He will tell you what is yet to come. He will glorify

Me because it is from Me that He will receive what He will make known to you."

"The thief does not come except to steal, and to kill and to destroy, I have come that they may have life, and that they may have it more abundantly."

John 10:10 (NKJV)

When you are in Christ, the abundant life and all its promises are for you. You have been made righteous. Jesus took your sins at the cross and gave you His righteousness. This is a beautiful exchange and gift from God! This is a free gift that God has made available to everyone who will just believe and receive His Son. When you do this, you are born into victory, born into authority, born into health, born into righteousness, and born into wisdom. A new covenant is established, and you become a member of the family of God. Can you believe it? Well, that is what the Bible says about you if choose to believe it or not. Many Christians do not have an understanding of who they are in Christ and therefore are not walking in the full manifestation of His promises. We receive this new identity by renewing our mind in the Word of God. We must stop believing what the world says or what the people around us are saying. Satan will try to keep you distracted and focused on other things. Because of this, we are missing out on the beautiful promises that belong to those in Christ. It is not enough to just hear the Word; you must believe it and declare the Word of the Lord.

"If you will not believe, surely you will not
be established."

Isaiah 7:9b (NKJV)

You have to have a foundation! If the Word says it, believe it! Don't forget that in 2 Peter 1:4a (NKJV) it says, "by which have been given to us exceedingly great and precious promises." Colossians 2:3 (NKJV) says, "In Whom are hidden all the treasures of wisdom and knowledge." Where? Wisdom and knowledge are found in Jesus. Satan will steal your identity if you do not know who you are. Some traditions of men will be a snare to you if you don't know the truth. The Bible even talks about that:

"Making the Word of God of no effect through
your tradition which you have handed down. And
many such things you do."

Mark 7:13 (NKJV)

"Beware lest any man cheat you through philosophy and empty deceit, according to the tradition
of men, according to the basic principles of the
world, and not according to Christ."

Colossians 2:8 (NKJV)

In 1 Corinthians 2:16b, it says that we have the mind of Christ. The Spirit of God will reveal what belongs to you, and He does this through His Holy Spirit. Learning about our identity of who we are in Christ is essential. If you want to learn more about your identity in Christ, Andrew Wommack has a book called *Spirit, Soul and Body*. It is an excellent book that teaches in depth your new identity of who you really are in Christ. This is just the beginning, let the Holy Spirit lead you through the Word of God and show you who you are. Get ready to see yourself in a whole new light. After you spend time in the following verses, we will then continue on our journey with learning about the Baptism of the Holy Spirit.

Who We Are in Christ Bible Verses

All verses are taken out of the New King James Version.

Who are you?

I am a child of God.

"Behold what manner of love the Father has bestowed on us, that we should be called the children of God!" (1 John 3:1a).

"The Spirit Himself bears witness with our spirit that we are the children of God, and if children, then heirs—heirs of God and joint heirs with Christ, if indeed we suffer with Him, that we may also be glorified together" (Romans 8:16-17).

I am sanctified.

"Sanctify them by Your truth. Your Word is truth" (John 17:17).

I am reconciled.

"Now all things are of God, who has reconciled us to Himself through Jesus Christ, and has given us the ministry of reconciliation" (2 Corinthians 5:18).

I am anointed.

"The Spirit of the Lord God is upon Me, because the Lord has anointed Me to preach good tidings to the poor; He has sent Me to heal the brokenhearted, to proclaim liberty to the captives, and the opening of the prison to those who are bound" (Isaiah 61:1).

I am forgiven and justified.

"Therefore let it be known to you, brethren, that through this Man [Jesus] is preached to you the forgiveness of sins; and by Him everyone who believes is justified from all things from which you could not be justified by the law of Moses" (Acts 13:38-39).

"Therefore, having been justified by faith, we have peace with God through our Lord Jesus Christ, through whom also we have access by faith into this grace in which we stand, and rejoice in hope of the glory of God" (Romans 5:1-2).

I am accepted.

"To the praise of the glory of His grace, by which He made us accepted in the Beloved" (Ephesians 1:6).

I have an inheritance.

"In Him also we have obtained an inheritance, being predestined according to the purpose of Him who works all things according to the counsel of His will" (Ephesians 1:11).

I am God's workmanship.

"For we are His workmanship, created in Christ Jesus for good works, which God prepared beforehand that we should walk in them" (Ephesians 2:10).

I am a new creation in Christ.

"Therefore, if anyone is in Christ, he is a new creation; old things have become new" (2 Corinthians 5:17).

I am heard.

"Then you will call upon Me and go and pray to Me, and I will listen to you. And you will seek Me and find Me, when you search for Me with all your heart" (Jeremiah 29:12-13).

"For the eyes of the Lord are on the righteous and His ears are open to their prayers, but the face of the Lord is against those who do evil" (I Peter 3:12).

Baptism in the Holy Spirit

Chapter Four

It's absolutely wonderful to be born again and forgiven of our sins, but God has more for us. Jesus Himself did not manifest the power of God until He had been baptized by the Spirit after His water baptism.

> "When He had been baptized, Jesus came up immediately from the water; and behold, the heavens were opened to Him, and He saw the Spirit of God descending like a dove and alighting upon Him. And suddenly a voice came from heaven, saying, 'This is My beloved Son, in whom I am well pleased.'"
>
> **Matthew 3:16-17 (NKJV)**

The baptism in the Holy Spirit served as the turning point from natural to supernatural in Christ's life. Jesus did not walk in power, heal the sick, or raise anyone from the dead until after this baptism in the Spirit took place. If the sinless Son of God was baptized in the Holy Spirit before beginning His ministry, don't you think it would be important for us? We will never walk in the fullness of God's promises and His abundance without this. You can be saved and on your way to heaven, but by not being filled or baptized in the Spirit, you are only receiving half of your gift. Salvation saves and the baptism in the Holy Spirit empowers! Jesus commanded His disciples not to do anything until they had been baptized in the Holy Spirit.

> ""And being assembled together with them, He commanded them not to depart from Jerusalem, but to wait for the promise of the Father, 'which,' He said, 'you have heard from Me; for John truly baptized with water, but you shall be baptized with the Holy Spirit not many days from now.'"

Acts 1:4-5 (NKJV)

> ""But you shall receive power when the Holy Spirit has come upon you; and you shall be witnesses to Me in Jerusalem, and in all Judea and Samaria, and to the end of the earth.'"

Acts 1:8-9 (NKJV)

If you are born again, the Holy Spirit takes up residence within you. Many Christians receive Jesus, but do not actually receive or acknowledge the Holy Spirit. To receive means to take or acquire; (something given, offered, or transmitted) get.[4] The Holy Spirit has so much more and wants to work through us with His power. The way this happens is by asking Him to baptize you with His power. This baptism is like

4 The American Heritage Dictionary, 2nd edition (Boston Massachusetts, Houghton Mifflin Company, 1985), 1032.

a river in you flowing out of you to give life to others. You literally become the hands and feet of Jesus.

I asked for the baptism of the Holy Spirit when I was around twelve years old. I was told that I needed this baptism, but no one really explained to me what it meant. I prayed with a friend of my mom who worked at a Christian television station. I felt nothing and did not pray in my heavenly language until my late twenties. I have since learned that you can be baptized in the Spirit without praying in tongues. Tongues is just the evidence that you have been baptized. When you pray and ask the Father to baptize you in the Spirit, receive it by faith. Even though I prayed in the Spirit, I did not totally understand what or who I possessed. Nor was I able to explain it to others. At times, I would have questions like, maybe it is not real or maybe I made it up? I even asked a pastor friend if I was actually baptized in the Spirit? I prayed in front of her, and she said, "Oh no, honey, that is real." I share this to show you that many people may have the same questions as I did. I grew up in a family that really did not understand this. As a result, through the years, I have had to read books, and ask questions to build my foundation to be able to explain it to others. I am now realizing that being baptized in the Spirit is the power of God being released through you. I believe this is why the enemy fights so many believers in this area.

Jesus says in John 14:12 (NKJV):

> "Most assuredly, I say to you, he who believes in Me, the works that I do he will do also; and greater works than these he will do, because I go to My Father."

To do greater works than Jesus did, we must be baptized with His Spirit. Understanding how loved we are and who we are in Him all work together to allow the power of Jesus to flow through us. Can you see how all this is linked together? God is not holding out on us. He has so much and is waiting for us to rise up and realize who we are. Being baptized in the Holy Spirit is a key to receiving all that God has for you. It also helps what God has put in you to flow out of you to others.

When you have been baptized and pray in the Spirit, you will begin to see the Word of God differently. Many people are saved (but not actually baptized in the Spirit), and they are unable to see that there is more to faith than just an act of believing. You can be a Christian, but not filled with His power. The baptism in the Holy Spirit makes God's power available to you. You will experience more and more victory in your life as you draw out this power of the Holy Spirit by faith. The baptism in the Holy Spirit is a gift, it is not something you earn or have to wait for. God tells us in the book of Luke to ask Him for the Holy Spirit.

"If you then, though you are evil, know how to give good gifts to your children, how much more will your Father in heaven give the Holy Spirit to those who ask Him!"

Luke 11:13 (NIV)

If you are hungry for more of God, ask Him to baptize you with His Holy Spirit. Pray this prayer with me:

Father, I surrender to You completely. I recognize my need for Your power to live the Christian life. According to your Word, it says that you will give the Holy Spirit to those who ask. I am asking and receiving this free gift of the Holy Spirit in Jesus Name, Amen.

Thank God for this gift and believe that you have received it.

"Therefore I say to you, whatever things you ask when you pray, believe that you receive them, and you will have them."

Mark 11:24 (NKJV)

Why is receiving the baptism of the Holy Spirit important? I can give you five reasons why we pray in tongues or, some would say, pray in the Spirit:

1. Helps you to pray

"In the same way, the Spirit helps us in our weakness. We do not know what we ought to pray for, but the Spirit himself intercedes for us through wordless groans" (Romans 8:26, NIV).

2. Reveals hidden treasures and mysteries of God

"However, we speak wisdom among those who are mature, yet not the wisdom of this age, nor of the rulers of this age, who are coming to nothing. But we speak the wisdom of God in a mystery, the hidden wisdom which God ordained before the ages for our glory" (1 Corinthians 2:6-7, NKJV).

"For anyone who speaks in a tongue does not speak to people but to God. Indeed, no one understands them; they utter mysteries by the Spirit" (1 Corinthians 14:2, NIV).

3. Edifies you

"Anyone who speaks in a tongue edifies themselves, but the one who prophesies edifies the church" (1 Corinthians 14:4, NIV).

4. Keeps us in the love of God

"But you, dear friends, by building yourselves up in your most holy faith and praying in the Holy Spirit. Keep yourselves in God's love as you wait for the mercy of our

Lord Jesus Christ to bring you to eternal life" (Jude 1:20-21, NIV).

5. Gives you rest and refreshing

"Very well then, with foreign lips and strange tongues God will speak to this people. To whom he said, 'This is the resting place, let the weary rest. This is the place of repose but they would not listen'" (Isaiah 28:11-12, NIV).

To further your studies on this subject, here are a few of my favorite books on this topic:

The New You & the Holy Spirit by Andrew Wommack

The God I Never Knew by Robert Morris

The Dynamic Duo, The Holy Spirit & You
by Rick Renner

Additional Verses about the Baptism in the Holy Spirit

"[John the Baptist speaking] 'I baptize you with water for repentance. But after me will come one who is more powerful than I, whose sandals I am not fit to carry. He will baptize you with the Holy Spirit and with fire'" (Matthew 3:11; Luke 3:16, NIV).

"I baptize you with water, but He will baptize you with the Holy Spirit" (Mark 1:8, NIV).

"Peter replied, 'Repent and be baptized, every one of you, in the Name of Jesus Christ for the forgiveness of your sins. And you will receive the gift of the Holy Spirit. The promise is for you and your children and for all who are afar off- for all whom the Lord our God will call'" (Acts 2:38-39, NIV).

"There he found some disciples and asked them, 'Did you receive the Holy Spirit when you believed?'" (Acts 19:1b-2, NIV).

"When Paul placed his hands on them, the Holy Spirit came on them, and they spoke in tongues and prophesied" (Acts 19:6, NIV).

"While Peter was still speaking these words, the Holy Spirit came on all who heard the message. The circumcised believers who had come with Peter were astonished that the gift of the Holy Spirit had been poured out even on Gentiles. For they heard them speaking in tongues and praising God" (Acts 10:44-46, NIV).

"Therefore, my brothers and sisters, be eager to prophesy, and do not forbid speaking in tongues" (1 Corinthians 14:39, NIV).

"If you then, though you are evil, know how to give good gifts to your children, how much more will your Father in heaven give the Holy Spirit to those who ask Him!" (Luke 11:13, NIV).

We Are the Righteousness of Christ

Chapter Five

"For I am not ashamed of the gospel of Christ, for it is the power of God to salvation for everyone who believes, for the Jew first and also for the Greek. For in it the righteousness of God is revealed from faith to faith; as it is written, 'The just shall live by faith.'"

Romans 1:16-17 (NKJV)

What is the gospel? It is the good news of what God has done for us through the death, burial, and resurrection of Christ. It is the power of God to salvation. The gospel empowers God to work salvation in the lives who will believe and receive it. The Gospel shows us who we are in Christ Jesus. Whoever believes in Christ and receives what He did is made righteous!

"Being justified freely by His grace through the redemption that is in Christ Jesus."

Romans 3:24 (NKJV)

Because of Jesus and what He did for us, our payment for sin has been paid in full. Jesus took our sins upon Himself and carried them to the cross. He offered us the exchange. He took our sin and gave us His righteousness. When God sees us, He sees us through Jesus, because we are in Him. We are made righteous through faith in Christ and His finished work on the Cross. This is a gift for all of us to receive, it has nothing to do with our performance or how good we think we are. We cannot add to it or subtract from it. Because our sins have been paid for by the precious blood of Jesus, we live justified.

> "Who was delivered up [Jesus] because of our offenses, and was raised because of our justification."
>
> **Romans 4:25 (NKJV)**

To justify means to demonstrate or prove to be just, right or valid. To declare free of blame; absolve. To free (man) of guilt and penalty attached to grievous sin.[5] We live free through Jesus! We are at one with God because of the payment that was made at the cross.

> "For if by the one man's offense death reigned through one (Adam) much more those who receive abundance of grace and of the gift of righteousness will reign in life through the one, Jesus Christ."
>
> **Romans 5:17 (NKJV)**

---

5 The American Heritage Dictionary, 2nd Edition (Boston Massachusetts, Houghton Mifflin Company, 1985), 695.

We are now to reign in this earthly life through the abundance of grace and the gift of righteousness. This again goes back to who we are in Christ. This is for those who receive what Jesus did at the cross, through His death, burial and resurrection.

> "For God so loved the world that He gave His one and only begotten Son, that whoever believes in Him should not perish but have everlasting life."

John 3:16 (NKJV)

You come into right standing with God by receiving His Son Jesus. God has so many promises for His sons and daughters. Understanding the love of God and who we are in Christ, we are made righteous when we receive Jesus as Lord. Repent and turn from doing life on your own and receive all that Jesus paid for by the shedding of His blood. Give Him your sins, and He will give you His righteousness.

Now, if you have made that exchange and received Jesus as your Lord and Savior, let me show you some of the promises that I have found in the Word of God for those who walk in His righteousness. Use the following pages of the promises as a reference for you to realize what now belongs to you. I know that there are many verses, but I wanted to show you how much God loves and longs for you to receive from Him. So read the verses and declare them over yourself and your family. This is where renewing your mind in the

Word of God is so important. I did not see all the promises until I read them back-to-back. God is not holding out on us. We just did not understand what was ours in Christ. Soak in the verses and receive all God has for you.

Jehovah Tsidkenu = The Lord is our righteousness

The following verses are taken out of the book of Proverbs, New International Version Bible

4:18 – "The path of the righteous is like the morning sun, shining ever brighter till the full light of day."

8:20-21 – "I walk in the way of righteousness, along the paths of justice, bestowing a rich inheritance on those who love me and making their treasuries full."

10:7a – "The name of the righteous is used in blessings."

10:11a – "The mouth of the righteous is a fountain of life."

10:16a – "The wages of the righteous is life."

10:21a – "The lips of the righteous nourish many."

10:24 – "What the wick dreads will overtake him, what the righteous desire will be granted."

10:30a – "The righteous will never be uprooted."

10:31a – "From the mouth of the righteous comes the fruit of wisdom."

10:32a – "The lips of the righteous know what finds favor."

11:5 – "The righteousness of the blameless makes their paths straight."

11:6 – "The righteousness of the upright delivers them."

11:8 – "The righteous person is rescued from trouble."

11:10 – "When the righteous prosper, the city rejoices."

11:19 – "Truly the righteous attain life."

11:23 – "The desire of the righteous ends only in good."

11:28b – "But the righteous will thrive like a green leaf."

11:30a – "The fruit of the righteous is a tree of life."

12:3b – "But the righteous cannot be uprooted."

12:5a – "The plans of the righteous are just."

12:7b – "But the house of the righteous stands firm."

12:21 – "No harm overtakes the righteous."

12:26a – "The righteous choose their friends carefully."

12:28 – "In the way of righteousness there is life; along that path is immortality."

13:5 – "The righteous hate what is false."

13:6a – "The righteousness guards the person of integrity."

13:9 – "The light of the righteous shines brightly."

13:21b – "But the righteous are rewarded with good things."

13:22b – "But a sinner's wealth is stored up for the righteous."

13:25 – "The righteous eat to their hearts content."

14:32a – "But even in death the righteous seek refuge in God."

14:34 – "Righteousness exalts a nation."

15:6 – "The house of the righteous contains great treasures, but the income of the wicked brings ruin."

15:9 – "The Lord detests the way of the wicked but He loves those who pursue righteousness."

15:28a – "The heart of the righteous weighs its answers."

15:29 – "The Lord is far from the wicked but He hears the prayers of the righteous."

16:8 – "Better a little with righteousness than much gain with injustice."

16:31 – "Grey hair is a crown of splendor; it is attained in the way of righteousness."

18:10 – "The name of the Lord is a fortified tower; the righteous run to it and are safe."

20:7 – "The righteous man leads a blameless life; blessed are their children after them."

21:12 – "The righteous one takes note of the house of the wicked and brings the wicked to ruin."

21:18 – "The wicked become a ransom for the righteous, and the unfaithful for the upright."

21:21 – "Whoever pursues righteousness and love finds life, prosperity and honor."

21:26 – "But the righteous give without sparing."

23:24 – "The father of a righteous child has great joy; a man who fathers a wise son rejoices in him."

24:16 – "For though a righteous man falls seven times, they rise again, but the wicked stumble when calamity strikes."

28:1b – "But the righteous are as bold as a lion."

29:2 – "When the righteous thrive, the people rejoice; when the wicked rule, the people groan."

29:16 – "When the wicked thrive, so does sin, but the righteous will see their downfall."

29:27 – "The righteous detest the dishonest; the wicked detest the upright."

Righteousness Verses outside of the Book of Proverbs

"For the Lord God is a sun and shield; The Lord will give grace and glory; no good thing will He withhold from those who walk uprightly" (Psalm 84:11, NKJV).

"But the mercy of the Lord is from everlasting to everlasting on those who fear Him, and his righteousness with their children's children. To such as keep His covenant, and to those who remember His commandments to do them" (Psalm 103:17-18 NKJV).

"The fruit of righteousness will be peace; its effect will be quietness and confidence forever" (Isaiah 32:17, NIV).

"All your children shall be taught by the Lord and great shall be peace of your children. In righteousness you shall be established; you shall be far from oppression, for you shall not fear; and from terror, for it shall not come near you" (Isaiah 54:13-14, NKJV).

"No weapons formed against you shall prosper, and every tongue which rises against you in judgment you shall condemn. This is the heritage of the servant of the Lord, and their righteousness is from Me, says the Lord" (Isaiah 54:17, NKJV).

"Being filled with the fruits of righteousness which are by Jesus Christ, to the glory and praise of God" (Philippians 1:11, NKJV).

"For in the Gospel a righteousness from God is revealed, a righteousness that is by faith from the first to the last, just as it is written: The righteous will live by faith'" (Romans 1:17, NIV).

"Behold, I long for your precepts; revive me in your righteousness" (Psalm 119:40, NKJV).

"The eyes of the Lord are on the righteous, and His ears are attentive to their cry. The righteous cry out, and the Lord hears, and delivers them from all their troubles" (Psalm 34:15, 17, NKJV).

"Tell the righteous it will be well with them, for they will enjoy the fruit of their deeds" (Isaiah 3:10, NIV).

"Abram believed the Lord, and He credited it to him as righteousness" (Genesis 15:6, NIV).

"For Christ is the end of the law for righteousness to everyone who believes" (Romans 10:4, NKJV).

"Do not My words do good to him who walks uprightly?" (Micah 2:7b, AMP).

"But we who live by the Spirit eagerly wait to receive by

faith the righteousness God has promised to us" (Galatians 5:5, NLT).

"As for me, I will see Your face in righteousness; I shall be satisfied when I awake in Your likeness" (Psalm 17:15, NKJV).

"Surely the righteous will never be shaken; they will be remembered forever. They will have no fear of bad news; their hearts are steadfast, trusting in the Lord. Their hearts are secure; they will have no fear; in the end they will look in triumph on their foes. They have freely scattered their gifts to the poor, their righteousness endures forever, their horn will be lifted high in honor" (Psalm 112:6-9, NIV).

"The righteous person may have many troubles, but the Lord delivers them from all their troubles" (Psalm 34:19, NIV).

"Sow righteousness for yourselves, reap the fruit of un-failing love, and break up your unplowed ground; for it is time to seek the Lord until He comes and showers His righteousness on you" (Hosea 10:12, NIV).

"For He made Him [Jesus] who knew no sin to be sin for us, that we might become the righteousness of God in Him" (2 Corinthians 5:21, NKJV).

"And do not present your members as instruments of un-righteousness to sin, but present yourselves to God as being alive from the dead, and your members as instruments of righteousness to God" (Romans 6:13, NKJV).

Wow! Did you realize that there were so many verses that talked about the promises for the righteous? This is just the beginning to get you started, there are many more promises to receive. In the next chapter, I would like to explain what it means to fear the Lord and the many wonderful promises that are for those who do.

Are you starting to see what belongs to you as a child of God? God the Father, from the beginning, wanted a family to commune with. The desire of His heart was to walk and talk with you daily, just like He did with Adam and Eve in the garden. Being in a loving relationship with you has always been God's plan from the beginning.

Renew your mind on the verses of how much God loves you. As you do, you will begin to see who you are in Him. God sees you as the righteousness of Christ! God loves you as much as He loves Jesus! He wants you to open the gifts that He has given to you through receiving Jesus and all the promises that are yes and amen! I leave you with a quote from Pastor Robert Morris from Gateway church:

"The key is to have faith, to believe God at His Word. And the more we receive the Word of God into our hearts and minds, the more our faith will be increased, and we'll be willing to believe Him and follow Him."

The Awesome Promises to Those Who Fear the Lord

Chapter Six

As I have been on this journey seeking the Lord and His Word, I have found many promises that belong to God's children. If you are a born-again believer in Jesus Christ, these are for you! I began to find all these verses that talked about the fear of the Lord. Many verses, as you will see, come with a promise. However, in order to walk in these promises, we must understand how to walk in a healthy fear of the Lord. What does it actually mean to fear the Lord?

To fear the Lord, means to have a right relationship, based on reverence and respect for God and His commands. It means to worship and be in awe of Him. The Old Testament Hebrew word for awe translates into fear, terror, or dread. How can this be? Should we be afraid of God? I began to see that it is a matter of what is in a person's heart. Rick Renner says it this way in his book, *A Life Ablaze*: "There are spiritual laws that must be obeyed if you want to be blessed. If you respect and handle God's Word and His power correctly, you will receive great blessings as a result. But if you choose to disobey, ignore, sidestep, or disrespect

His truth, His presence, and His power, the same power that could help you may bring you a severe correction or even judgement" (Renner 422).

> "Let us hear the conclusion of the whole matter: Fear God and keep His commandments, for this is man's all. For God will bring every work into judgement, including every secret thing, whether good or evil."

Ecclesiastes 12:13-14 (NKJV)

Remember that God is holy, and we must never forget that. He is worthy of our worship and praise. God so desires to be in a personal relationship with you, and He wants to bless you. However, again, we need to check our heart and motives. Have you ever been in a relationship with someone that is one-sided? You pour your heart into that person, and they keep asking for more of your time, resources, and energy, but nothing is given back in return? Don't let your relationship with God be one-sided. Remember, being in a relationship takes two!

God so desires for you to get to know Him. The Word of God is full of promises for those who reverently fear Him. Let's look at a few verses and the promises that come with them.

> "The fear of the Lord is the beginning of wisdom, and knowledge of the Holy One is understanding."

Proverbs 9:10 (NKJV)

Many of us are asking God for wisdom over our lives, situations, and for decisions that have to be made. However, in this verse, it says that the beginning of wisdom and knowledge come by fearing the Lord and being in a relationship with Him. Well, you might be saying, "How does someone have a relationship with God?" I would ask you, "How do you have a relationship with a friend?" You would spend time and get to know them. You would talk with and listen to the person. Might I say that you would schedule a time to meet? This is the same way that you would get to know God. You were created to be in fellowship with Him. He wanted a family to commune with! He created Adam and Eve in the garden, and, before they chose to sin, God walked and talked with them. Because they disobeyed God, they disconnected from this relationship with Him. When Jesus died on the cross, He was the ultimate sacrifice. Jesus paid the price for sin, and because of this, He restored our ability to have access to Father God. God wanted the relationship with His people restored and this is one of the reasons He sent His Son Jesus. Our relationship with God is what brings Him to walk with us, as He did with Adam and Eve.

Let's look at more verses about those who fear the Lord and the promises that follow.

"Who then are those who fear the Lord? He will instruct them in the ways they should choose. They will spend their days in prosperity and their descendants will inherit the land. The Lord confides in those who fear Him: He makes His covenant known to them."

Psalm 25:12-14 (NIV)

Again, we are asking God for wisdom, but it starts with knowing Him. The verses above state that when we fear the Lord, He will instruct us in the way chosen for us. How many times have you heard someone say, "I don't know what to do" or "I don't know what my purpose is"? God knows, and this verse tells us that He will instruct you in the way chosen for you. How cool is that? The verses continue to say that the person who fears the Lord will spend his days in prosperity and his descendants will inherit the land. What does prosperity mean? I am glad you asked. According to the American Heritage Dictionary, it means the condition of being prosperous. And being prosperous is having success, flourishing, well to do, or well off.[6] God is for you and not against you.

"For you, God, have heard my vows; You have given me the heritage of those who fear Your Name."

Psalm 61:5 (NIV)

God has abundance that He wants to share. All He asks is that you get to know Him personally and obey Him. He said that He would confide in you and make His covenant known

---

6 The American Heritage Dictionary, 2nd Edition (Boston Massachusetts, Houghton Mifflin Company, 1985), 995.

to you. Are you looking for direction? Look to God through His Word and watch what He will show you! Because of Jesus, we are under a new covenant. God will show you what belongs to you because of this new covenant.

> "By humility and the fear of the Lord are riches and honor and life."
>
> **Proverbs 22:4 (NKJV)**

This is a promise to those who are in relationship and in awe of God! Let's look at some more awesome and crazy good promises.

> "How joyful are those who fear the Lord and delight in obeying His commands. Their children will be successful everywhere; an entire generation of godly people will be blessed. They themselves will be wealthy, and their good deeds will last forever. Light shines in the darkness for the godly. They are generous, compassionate, and righteous."
>
> **Psalm 112:1-4 (NLT)**

Do you need joy? Here it says that we will be joyful when we fear God and delight in obeying His commands. Before I understood the promises of God, I thought the Bible was all these rules and regulations. God's Word is to give you direction to show you how to walk out this life. It is a secret treasure for you to find God's abundance and promises for you and your family. In John 10:10, it is the thief (Satan) that steals, kills, and destroys. Jesus came to give you an abundant life. When you start to see what is yours, you will begin to take back in the spiritual realm what Satan has stolen from you. I can tell you this with confidence because this is what is happening to me. I am tired of Satan taking what belongs to me as a daughter of God. I want back what is rightfully mine, in Jesus' Name. Amen.

Let's continue looking at this verse above. When we fear the Lord and obey His commands, it then says our children will be successful everywhere and entire generation of godly people will be blessed. If you want to bless your children, get in a right relationship with God. Worship and love Him and start speaking and believing this promise. Here, again in verse 3, it says that we will be wealthy, and their good deeds will last forever. The definition of wealthy is having wealth: affluent, richly supplied, abundant.[7] When you start to understand this concept, you will be given light from your Father in heaven while others walk in darkness. This is not because God wants people to stay in darkness, but it is because you are in awe of Him that His light will begin to show you things. Because of this love, you will become generous, compassionate, and righteous. God is in the business of blessing His kids, and it all starts with learning to fear Him and being in a relationship with Him. Should I keep going? I

---

7 The American Heritage Dictionary, 2nd Edition (Boston Massachusetts, Houghton Mifflin Company, 1985), 1369.

will state a few more verses to make sure that you are starting to see the awesome promises of God to those who fear Him.

"For as high as the heavens are above the earth, so great is His love for those who fear Him; as far as the east is from the west, so far has He removed our transgressions from us. As a father has compassion on his children, so the Lord has compassion on those who fear Him."

Psalm 103:11-13 (NIV)

Do you need to be loved? Do you need to feel like you belong somewhere? God has unfailing love that is endless to those that are in a relationship with Him. He will be a Father to you, if you will let Him in. Many people may not have had a good relationship with their earthly father, and as a result, they see God to be the same way. Don't believe the lies that God does not love you. Your heavenly Father is so in love with you. He wants to be tender and compassionate towards you. Because of Jesus and the complete work of the cross, our sins have been far removed from us. This is the unmerited favor of God. Jesus already paid for your sins on the cross. All your sins, past, present and future have been paid for. Receive this precious gift from God and let Him be your Father, your heavenly Father. Here is another cool verse that is a promise.

"The angel of the Lord encamps all around
those who fear Him and delivers them."

Psalm 34:7 (NIV)

Do you need God's protection? When you are walking
with God in relationship, this promise belongs to you. He
will give His angels charge over you and they will deliver
you if you believe His Word. Wow, the promises are endless
to those who fear God.

"He will be a sure foundation for your times, a
rich store of salvation and wisdom and knowledge; the fear of the Lord is the key to this treasure."

Isaiah 33:6 (NIV)

According to the American Heritage Dictionary "sure"
means certain, firm, sure of victory, bound to come about
or to happen, steady, reliable and safe.[8] I believe that God
is saying that He will be all these things to those people that
are in relationship with Him. Think about this verse. Do you
need a sure foundation for the times that we live in? Isaiah continues to say a rich store of salvation, wisdom, and
knowledge are yours when you fear the Lord. Beloved children of God, I hope your eyes are starting to open to the awesome promises to those who fear the Lord. Spending time
with God is never wasted. God wants to share all of these

---

8 The American Heritage Dictionary, 2nd Edition (Boston Massachusetts, Houghton Mifflin, Company, 1985), 1223.

promises with you and bless you. Grab a hold of this and renew your mind. Believe in your heart that these verses are for you! Put the Word of God into your heart and watch what God will do. Let's look at one more fear of the Lord verse.

> "Oh, how great is Your goodness, which You have laid up for those who fear You, which You have prepared for those who trust in You in the presence of the sons of men! You shall hide them in the secret place of Your presence from the plots of men; You shall keep them secretly in a pavilion from the strife of tongues."

Psalm 31:19-20 (NKJV)

How great is the goodness that God has laid up for those who fear Him. As a child of God, I hope you are beginning to see the beautiful promises for those that esteem God in awe and get to know Him. These are just a few verses on the fear of the Lord, there are more in the Word of God. Meditate on the fear of the Lord and allow the verses to take root deep within your heart. I pray that your eyes and heart will be open to the amazing promises that are for those who will just worship the Lord and be in relationship with Him.

If you have known that there is a God but have never made Him the Lord of your life, I am here to tell you that He wants a relationship with you. Ask Him into your heart.

"If you declare with your mouth that Jesus is
Lord and believe in your heart that God raised
him from the dead, you will be saved. For it is
with your heart that you believe and are justified,
and it is with your mouth that you profess your
faith and are saved."

Romans 10:9-10 (NIV)

All of these promises are yes and amen! God has amazing gifts stored up for His kids! Don't miss out on the beautiful promises that God has in store for those who fear Him.

"Fear the Lord, you His holy people, for those
who fear Him lack nothing."

Psalm 34:9 (NIV)

THE *fear* OF THE LORD

Additional Scriptures on the Fear of the Lord

All the following verses are taken from the New King James Version Bible unless noted.

"Oh, that they had such a heart in them that they would fear Me and always keep all My commandments, that it might be well with them and with their children forever!" (Deuteronomy 5:29).

"And to man He said, Behold the fear of the Lord, that is wisdom, and to depart from evil is understanding" (Job 28:28).

"Let all the earth fear the Lord; Let all the inhabitants of the world stand in awe of Him" (Psalm 33:8).

"Behold, the eye of the Lord is on those who fear Him, on those who hope in His mercy, to deliver their soul from death, and to keep them alive in famine" (Psalm 33:18-19).

"Come, you children, listen to Me; I will teach you the fear of the Lord" (Psalm 34:11).

"But the mercy of the Lord is from everlasting to everlasting on those who fear Him, and His righteousness to children's children, to such as keep His covenant, and to those who remember His commandments to do them" (Psalm 103:17-18).

"He has given food to this those who fear Him; He will ever be mindful of His covenant. He has declared to His people the power of His works, in giving them the heritage of the nations" (Psalm 111:5-6).

"The fear of the Lord is the beginning of wisdom; a good understanding have all those who do His commandments. His praise endures forever" (Psalm 111:10).

"You who fear the Lord, trust in the Lord; He is their help and their shield" (Psalm 115:11).

"He will bless those who fear the Lord, both small and great. May the Lord give you increase more and more, you and your children. May you be blessed by the Lord, who made heaven and earth" (Psalm 115:13-15).

"Blessed is everyone who fears the Lord, who walks in His ways. When you eat the labor of your hands, you shall be happy, and it shall be well with you. Your wife shall be like a fruitful vine in the very heart of your house, your children like olive plants all around your table. Behold, thus shall the man be blessed who fears the Lord" (Psalm 128:1-4).

"The Lord is near to all who call upon Him, to all who call upon Him in truth. He will fulfill the desire of those who fear Him; He also will hear their cry and save them"

(Psalm145:18-19).

"The Lord takes pleasure in those who fear Him, in those who hope in His mercy" (Psalm 147:11).

"The fear of the Lord is the beginning of knowledge, but fools despise wisdom and instruction" (Proverbs 1:7).

"The fear of the Lord is to hate evil; pride and arrogance and the evil way and the perverse mouth I hate" (Proverbs 8:13).

"The fear of the Lord prolongs days, but the years of the wicked will be shortened" (Proverbs 10:27).

"In the fear of the Lord there is strong confidence, and his children will have a place of refuge. The fear of the Lord is a fountain of life, to turn one away from the snares of death" (Proverbs 14:26-27).

"Confidence and strength flood the hearts of the lovers of God who live in awe of Him, and their devotion provides their children with a place of shelter and security" (Proverbs 14:26, TPT).

"The fear of the Lord is the instruction of wisdom, and before honor is humility" (Proverbs 15:33).

"The fear of the Lord leads to life, and he who has it will abide in satisfaction; He will not be visited with evil"

(Proverbs 19:23).

"And the Spirit of the Lord shall rest upon him, the Spirit of wisdom and understanding, the Spirit of counsel and might, the Spirit of knowledge and of the fear of the Lord" (Isaiah 11:2).

"Then those who feared the Lord spoke to one another, and the Lord listened and heard them; so a book of remembrance was written before Him for those who fear the Lord and meditate on His Name. 'They shall be Mine,' says the Lord of hosts, 'On that day that I make them My jewels. And I will spare them as a man spares his own son who serves him" (Malachi 3:16-17).

"And His mercy is on those who fear Him from generation to generation" (Luke 1:50).

God Our Provider

Chapter Seven

The Bible has a lot to say about prosperity, finances, and blessings. God has so much He wants to give His children, but we find it hard to surrender this area to Him. When we hang on to the money we make, we become our own provider in the place of God. We give God other areas of our lives, but our finances are a different story. I want to show you in the Word of God that, when you put Him first, He will become your provider. More than any other promises, this is an area that I have found scripture after scripture showing God's plan for blessing His kids. The Bible talks about this more than I think most people realize. Satan is trying to keep you ignorant of these promises. He does not want you to learn that God has already provided for you way above what you could ever dream of.

Through this chapter, I am going to give you a lot of scripture for you to meditate on and renew your mind in what God actually says. It was not until I read the verses over and over again, that I received the understanding and had a true revelation of the Word. God has given us His blueprints of how to live in His blessings and prosperity. Are you ready to see what the Bible has to say about living in the blessings and prosperity of God? Let us begin our journey and open our eyes to the truth of God's Word.

> "Bring all the tithes into the storehouse, that there may be food in My house. And try Me in this," says the Lord of hosts, "If I will not open for the windows of heaven and pour out for you such blessing that there will not be room enough to receive it. And I will rebuke the devourer for your sakes, so that he will not destroy the fruit of your ground, nor shall the vine fail to bear fruit for you in the field," says the Lord of hosts.

Malachi 3:10-11 (NKJV)

God actually tells us to test Him in this area. A tithe is a tenth of what comes to you. God is just asking you to honor Him with your substance that He has given you. He says give it to your storehouse. Your storehouse is your church, or where you are being fed the Word of God. When we give 10 percent of our earnings to God, we are learning to put Him first. I have learned that every area in which you choose to put God first, He will bless.

When I was nineteen, I did not understand why, but I had this desire to give to a Christian youth center in Joliet Illinois. It was through this center that I gave my life to Christ. This was the beginning of my journey with giving. I was so thankful for what God had done in my heart that I sowed into that youth center. God would nudge me to give to different ministries. It was like I knew I needed to do this, but I did not understand why. I would give five dollars here, then it increased each time I gave. This went on for some time. God would put in my heart to give a larger tithe to my church and offerings to other ministries. In my head, I would think, "God, that does not make sense." At this time, I was newly married, and we didn't have much. God began to stretch me more and more.

Let me clear up a misunderstanding that confuses people. The tithe is 10 percent of your income and goes to your church where you are being fed the Word of God. An offering is a gift that is above and beyond your tithe. An offering could be sown into another ministry that you are being blessed from or it could be given to an organization that is close to your heart. The last type of giving is alms. This is your gifts to the poor and needy. I believe it is important to know the difference and obey God's direction for each of these areas. I found that each time I obeyed the nudge in my heart, it was as if God would then show me in His Word why I was being led to give. Again, I did not see the magnitude of this until I walked in obedience. It was after that I began to see the Word like never before in this area. The Book of Proverbs is packed full of promises. Look what it says in Proverbs 8:17-21 (NLT):

"I love all who love me [wisdom]. Those who search will surely find me. I have riches and honor, as well as enduring wealth and justice. My gifts are better than fine gold, even the purest gold, my wages better than sterling silver! I walk in righteousness, in paths of justice. Those who love me inherit wealth. I will fill their treasuries."

I have learned that the Word is Jesus Himself. He is the wisdom that we seek. As we seek Jesus our wisdom, look at what is promised: riches, honor, enduring wealth, and prosperity. He is better than fine gold. The more we truly seek after Jesus and put Him first, then He makes our treasuries full.

"The godly are showered with blessings."

Proverbs 10:6a (NLT)

"The blessing of the Lord makes one rich, and He adds no sorrow with it."

Proverbs 10:22 (NKJV)

"One person gives freely, yet gains even more; another withholds unduly, but comes to poverty. A generous person will prosper; whoever refreshes others will be refreshed."

Proverbs 11:24-25 (NIV)

I challenge you to read the book of Proverbs, one chapter every day of the month. The more one renews their mind in the Word of God, the more they will see His promises that He has laid out for them. God is not holding out on you. We just need to surrender our heart to Him and trust that He will do what His Word says.

Another nugget I have learned is that those who give and take care of the poor, are ones God in turn, takes care of. You are giving unto the Lord when you share your substance with the needy. Here are a few verses to support this:

"If you help the poor, you are lending to the Lord and He will repay you!"

Proverbs 19:17 (NLT)

"Blessed are those who are generous, because they feed the poor."

Proverbs 22:9 (NLT)

"He who gives to the poor will not lack, but he who hides his eyes will have many curses."

Proverbs 28:27 (NKJV)

God is a loving God and is not a respecter of persons. I believe the difference is the heart of everyone. Are you putting God first in your finances, or are you tipping Him? Tithing and giving has not always been easy to do. At times, I thought to myself, "This is crazy! What am I doing?" With our natural instincts, it does not make sense. I have learned most of God's promises go against our natural thinking. As I walked in obedience, I would then discover more verses on His blessings and prosperity in His Word. Was I scared to tithe and give? Absolutely! God's way is bigger than our way. He is not trying to take something from you, but He is trying to give something to you. It may leave your hands, but it will never leave your life. Give to God because you are thankful for all He has done for you. Don't give to get but give to be a blessing. Keep your motives right before the Lord and watch what He will do. He promises in His Word that He will provide for us when we put Him first in our finances. Here are some more verses supporting this:

> "But seek first His Kingdom and His righteousness, and all these things will be given to you as well."

> **Matthew 6:33 (NIV)**

We are told to seek the kingdom of God and His righteousness, then all the other things will be given. Where is God when it comes to your finances? Do you honor Him, put Him first? The reason I use so many verses is to show you that it is better to give to God what belongs to God. He will then bless the rest.

> "The house of the righteous contains great treasure, but the income of the wicked brings ruin."

> **Proverbs 15:6 (NIV)**

When God is not first in this area, you could have it all and still have nothing. Money is not evil; it is the love of money that causes people issues. Make sure that God has first place in your life and finances. God is not trying to take from you or keep His blessings from you. He is waiting for you to take Him at His Word and put Him first. Whenever I think of all the promises of God, I picture God giving each one of us a gift. Some of us receive it, and some of us say thank you but never open it. And yet there are some that just put it on the shelf. How many gifts and promises are not being opened from our heavenly Father? I think many are going to be very disappointed when God shows them that He gave them everything. They just choose not to open His gifts. They did not take the time to read His Word or get to know Him. He has the blueprints of His promises that are for those that have chosen to receive His Son Jesus. Jesus paid for each of us and, because of what He did for us at the cross and resurrection, we can now receive all the promises. They have been paid for by the precious blood of Jesus. Wow, that is the beauty of the Word. The promises are not gained by anything that you do. You cannot earn them or pay for them. They are a gift for all to receive. We again, just need to surrender and receive them.

Renew your mind on the following list of verses that pertain to prosperity and blessings. There are more, but these are the ones that have made an impact on me. I challenge you to check your heart in the area of tithing and giving. Remember, when much is given to you, much is expected from you. God gives and blesses so that you can enjoy your life. But what is given to you is not all for you:

> "Command those who are rich in this present age not to be haughty, nor to trust in uncertain riches but in the living God, who gives us richly all things to enjoy. Let them do good works, ready to give, willing to share."

> **1 Timothy 6:17-18 (NKJV)**

God needs His people to prosper so that He can work through us and build His kingdom. We should be overflowing with God's blessing so that we could be a blessing to others. This is God's design. Put God first and know that He is your provider. Keep your heart right and watch God provide for you like you have never seen before.

Additional Verses Showing God as Our Provider

All the following verses are found in the New Kings James Version unless noted.

"Evil pursues the sinners, but to the righteous good shall be repaid. A good man leaves an inheritance to his children's children, but the wealth of the sinner is stored up for the righteous" (Proverbs 13:21-22).

"The house of the wicked will be overthrown, but the tent of the upright will flourish" (Proverbs 14:11).

"He who despises his neighbor sins, but he who has mercy on the poor, happy is he" (Proverbs 14:21).

"He who oppresses the poor reproaches his Maker, but he who honors Him has mercy on the needy" (Proverbs 14:31).

"He who heeds the Word wisely will find good, and whoever trusts in the Lord, happy is he" (Proverbs 16:20).

"A man's gift makes room for him, and brings him before great men" (Proverbs 18:16).

"The fear of the Lord leads to life, and he who has it will abide in satisfaction" (Proverbs 19:23).

"Whoever shuts his ears to the cry of the poor will also cry himself and not be heard" (Proverbs 21:13).

"He covets greedily all day long, but the righteous gives and does not spare" (Proverbs 21:26).

"By humility and the fear of the Lord are riches and honor and life" (Proverbs 22:4).

"He who covers his sins will not prosper, but whoever confesses and forsakes them will have mercy" (Proverbs 28:13).

"A faithful man will abound with blessings, but he who hastens to be rich will not go unpunished" (Proverbs 28:20).

"He who is of a proud heart stirs up strife, but he who trusts in the Lord will be prospered" (Proverbs 28:25).

"If they obey and serve Him, they shall spend their days in prosperity and their years in pleasures. But if they do not obey, they will perish by the sword and die without knowledge" (Job 36:11-12).

"Then Isaac sowed in that land and reaped in the same year a hundredfold, and the Lord blessed him. The man began to proser, and continued prospering until he became very prosperous" (Genesis 26:12-13).

"Therefore keep the words of this covenant, and do

them, that you may prosper in all that you do" (Deuteronomy 29:9).

"For God gives wisdom and knowledge and joy, to a man who is good in His sight; but to the sinner He gives the work of gathering and collecting, that he may give to him who is good before God" (Ecclesiastes 2:26ᵃ).

"Salvation belongs to the Lord. Your blessing is upon your people" (Psalm 3:8).

"But those who seek the Lord shall not lack any good thing" (Psalm 34:10b).

"For the Lord God is a sun and shield; The Lord will give grace and glory; no good thing will He withhold from those who walk uprightly" (Psalm 84:11).

"Remember me, Lord, when you show favor to your people; come near and rescue me. Let me share in the prosperity of your chosen ones. Let me rejoice in the joy of your people; let me praise you with those who are your heritage" (Psalm 106:4-5, NLT).

"Praise the Lord! How joyful are those who fear the Lord and delight in obeying His commands. Their children will be successful everywhere; an entire generation of godly people will be blessed. They themselves will be wealthy, and their good deeds will last forever. Light shines in the darkness for the godly. They are generous, compassionate, and righteous.

Good comes to those who lend money generously and conduct their business fairly" (Psalm 112:1-5, NLT).

"May the Lord give you increase more and more, you and your children. May you be blessed by the Lord, who made heaven and earth" (Psalm 115:14-15).

"I will give you the treasures of darkness, and hidden riches of secret places, that you may know that I am the Lord, who call you by your name, Am the God of Israel" (Isaiah 45:3).

"Beloved, I pray that you may prosper in all things and be in health, just as your soul prospers" (3 John 2).

"He [Uzziah] sought God in the days of Zechariah, who had understanding in the visions of God; and as long as he sought the Lord, God made him prosper" (2 Chronicles 26:5).

"Since the people began to bring the offerings into the house of the Lord, we have had enough to eat and have plenty left, for the Lord has blessed His people; and what is left is this great abundance" (2 Chronicles 31:10b).

"As for every man to whom God has given riches and wealth and given him power to eat of it, to receive his heritage and rejoice in his labor—this is a gift of God. For he will not dwell unduly on the days of his life, because God keeps him busy with the joy of his heart" (Ecclesiastes 5:19-20).

"Command those who are rich in this present age not to be haughty, nor to trust in uncertain riches, but in the living God, who gives us richly all things to enjoy. Let them do good, that they be rich in good works, ready to give, willing to share, storing up for themselves a good foundation for the time to come, that they may lay hold on eternal life" (1 Timothy 6:17-19).

"I was young and now I am old, yet I have never seen the righteous forsaken or their children begging for bread. They are always generous and lend freely; their children will be a blessing" (Psalm 37:25-26, NIV).

"He brought out his people with rejoicing, His chosen ones with shouts of joy; He gave them the lands of the nations, and they fell heir to what others had toiled for" (Psalm 105:43-44, NIV).

"For there is no difference between Jew or Gentile-the same Lord is Lord of all and richly blesses all who call on Him" (Romans 10:12, NIV).

"O Lord, You are my portion of my inheritance and my cup; you maintain my lot. The lines have fallen to me in pleasant places; Yes, I have a good inheritance" (Psalm 16:5-6).

"Surely, Lord, you bless the righteous; you surround them with Your favor as with a shield" (Psalm 5:12, NIV).

"Blessed be the Lord, who daily loads us with benefits,

the God of our salvation!" (Psalm 68:19).

"May the Lord, the God of your ancestors, increase you a thousand times and bless you as He has promised" (Deuteronomy 1:11, NIV).

"For you, O God, have heard my vows; You have given me the heritage of those who fear Your Name" (Psalm 61:5).

"Tell the righteous it will be well with them, for they will enjoy the fruit of their deeds" (Isaiah 3:10, NIV).

"The Lord will greatly bless His people wherever they plant seed, bountiful crops will spring up" (Isaiah 32:20a, NLT).

"But the godly are generous givers. The godly always give generous loans to others, and their children are a blessing" (Psalm 37:21b, 26; NLT).

"Some people are always greedy for more, but the godly love to give!" (Proverbs 21:26, NLT).

"Trust in your money and down you go! But the godly flourish like leaves in spring" (Proverbs 11:28, NLT).

"Then he said, 'Beware!' Guard against every kind of greed. Life is not measured by how much you own" (Luke 12:15, NLT).

"Yes, a person is a fool to store up earthly wealth but not have a rich relationship with God" (Luke 12:21, NLT).

"He told me [angel], 'Cornelius, your prayer has been heard, and your gifts to the poor have been noticed by God!'" (Acts 10:31).

"Those who are taught the Word of God should provide for their teachers, sharing all good things with them. Don't be misled—you cannot mock the justice of God. You will always harvest what you plant" (Galatians 6:6-7, NLT).

Blessings Down to a Thousand Generations

Chapter Eight

As we continue on our journey, have you ever thought of praying for your future generations? I came across some verses years ago that inspired me to do just that. I want to be known as that great, great grandmother that prayed for her future grandchildren. I want to leave a legacy and I have learned the power of the Word of God allows you to do just that.

"But as for me and my house, we will serve The Lord."

Joshua 24:15b (NKJV)

Because of my own journey and learning that my previous generations in my family were not Christians, I desired to build a spiritual foundation for my generations after me. Here are just a few verses that caught my attention speaking about a thousand generations.

"May the Lord, the God of your ancestors, increase you a thousand times and bless you as He has promised!"

Deuteronomy 1:11 (NIV)

> "Know therefore that the Lord your God is God;
> He is the faithful God, keeping His covenant of
> love to a thousand generations of those who love
> Him and keep His commandments."

Deuteronomy 7:9 (NIV)

God loves you so much that His desire is to continue His covenant of love down through your generations. Isn't that amazing? A covenant is defined as:[9]

1. A binding agreement made by two or more persons or parties
2. A formal sealed agreement or contract
3. A suit to recover damages for violation of such a contract
4. To promise by a covenant

His love never fails. I believe that many of us really don't understand unconditional love or the God kind of love. I did not. I had to allow God to heal my heart and show me what true love was. As I started to receive this love from God, I began to see myself differently. Did you know that the love of God drives out fear?

> "There is no fear in love; but perfect love casts
> out fear, because fear involves torment. But he
> who fears has not been made perfect in love."

1 John 4:18 (NKJV)

---

9 The American Heritage Dictionary, 2nd Edition (Boston Massachusetts, Houghton Mifflin Company, 1985), 334.

Let the love of God perfect you. You are no longer a slave to fear.

"For God has not given us a spirit of fear, but of power and of love and of a sound mind."

2 Timothy 1:7 (NKJV)

My desire is for the future generations to grab hold of this. Here is another cool verse.

"He always stands by His covenant, the commitment He made to a thousand generations."

Psalm 105:8 (NLT)

God is a good God. He has already set this into motion. The enemy is the one who is stealing, killing, and destroying you and your family. Jesus came to give you life and not just life but life in abundance.

"The thief does not come except to steal, and to kill, and to destroy. I have come that they may have life, and that they may have it more abundantly."

John 10:10 (NKJV)

We need to renew our minds in the truth of what the Word says and not what society tells us. There is power in our words! Life and death are in the power of our tongue.

"Death and life are in the power of the tongue,
and those who love it will eat its fruit."

Proverbs 18:21 (NKJV)

We will either speak life over our children and future generations or we will speak death. The second part of the verse says, and those who love it will eat its fruit. What you say is so important. Why would you want to speak death and eat the yuk of your words? There is delicious fruit to have when we line up our words with God's Word. I want to plant life in the generations to come. What you sow is what you reap. Let's make a decision to speak what God says. Here is another powerful truth.

"But the posterity of the righteous will be delivered."

Proverbs 11:21b (NKJV)

The definition of posterity means future generations, all of a person's descendants.[10] After learning that I am the righteousness of Christ because of what He did for me, I can now declare that all my future generations will be delivered because I am in Christ. God is not just after a relationship with you, He wants all of your future generations. Now that truly

10 The American Heritage Dictionary, 2nd Edition (Boston Massachusetts, Houghton Mifflin Company, 1985), 698.

shows you the love of God! This is all available to those that are in a relationship with God and grab hold of the promises. Speak them over your family and believe them. Even if you have children that are not walking with the Lord. Start praying and declaring these verses and watch what the power of the Word of God will do. Satan is trying get you to believe a lie to steal from your generations. Not in my house, my prayer is that I would not lose one. You may be saying, "Oh Tammy, you are stretching this a little far." My question to you is, "What harm am I doing?" I will learn when I get to heaven if I am off. But what if I am right and it was in front of us all along? Let the Spirit speak to your heart and discover what is already yours. Remember the gifts that we talked about in previous pages. We all have these gifts from God if we belong to Him. All we need to do is receive and open them. Our world is turning upside down and the future generations are depending on us older saints to get these promises deep down in our hearts and out of our mouths. The future generations are depending on us to set the stage for them. This is a verse that I just love, and I speak it over my children every day.

"'As for Me,' says the Lord, 'This is my covenant with them; My spirit who is upon you and My words which I have put in your mouth, shall not depart from your mouth, nor from the mouth of your descendants, nor from your descendant descendants, says the Lord, from this time and forevermore.'"

Isaiah 59:21 (NKJV)

That's a lot of generations. Here is another one that is amazing.

"But the mercy of the Lord is from everlasting to everlasting on those who fear Him, and His righteousness to children's children. To such as keep His covenant and those who remember His commandments to do them."

Psalm 103:17-18 (NKJV)

God's Word is so amazing, and it is packed full of His promises. As a child of God, it is time for us to start understanding all that has been given to us. Be a vessel for God to work through and believe His Word for this next generation. Are you willing to take a stand for your future generations? Don't just read them but declare and stand on them. Trust in God and His love for you and your future generations. The following verses are for you to see that God is about future generations:

"Our children will also serve Him. Future generations will hear about the wonders of the Lord" (Psalm 22:30, NLT).

"May the Lord richly bless both you and your children. May you be blessed by the Lord, who made heaven and earth" (Psalm 115:14-15, NLT).

"I will pour out My Spirit on your descendants and My

blessing on your children" (Isaiah 44:3b, NLT).

"The godly walk with integrity; blessed are their children who follow them" (Proverbs 20:7, NLT).

"For He has strengthened the bars of your gates and blessed your children within your walls" (Psalm 147:13, NLT).

"Those who fear the Lord are secure; He will be a refuge for their children" (Proverbs 14:26, NLT).

"Oh, that they had such a heart in them that they would fear Me, and always keep all My commandments, that it might be well with them and their children forever!" (Deuteronomy 5:29, NKJV).

"And you and your children and grandchildren must fear the Lord your God as long as you live. If you obey all His decrees and commands, you will enjoy a long life" (Deuteronomy 6:2, NLT).

"He shows mercy from generation to generation to all who fear Him" (Luke 1:50, NLT).

"All your children shall be taught by the Lord, and great shall be the peace of your children" (Isaiah 54:13, NKJV).

Promises for Your Family

Chapter Nine

Now let's look at the promises God has in store for your family. As I have said before, I did not come out of a strong Christian home. I had a lot of drama and crisis throughout my life. My parents' marriage was not stable, and my father struggled with mental health issues. I would pray and seek God for restoration and healing in my family. Through this painful journey, I began to find a lot of the verses that talked about family. I began to write and speak the verses out loud. These verses became a lifeline for me. At the time, I thought that I was the only one going through family issues. Oh, how wrong I was to believe this. I realize that every family has something that they are going through. I hope to build your confidence and give you tools to be able to speak/declare over your loved ones. You may not be able to change individuals, but prayer moves mountains. In my own life, I have had to let go of situations and trust God to move in the person's life. I gained the strength to do so, through His Word.

Just like the last chapter in praying for your future generations, you can speak the promises of God over your family. Remember, life and death are in the power of your tongue. The more you speak life into your family, the more you are planting seed. Eventually that seed will grow if we do not give up. I personally have wanted to give up at times. Things in my life seemed to get worse. But God continued to show me in His Word, promises that belonged to His children that are in Christ. The more I spoke His Word the more I would begin to see what was mine. Even though at times, I could not see past the crisis in my family, I knew in my heart that the Word of God was my answer. I have talked to and prayed for many people that have heartache from family issues. Most of the time, they are issues that are out of their control. The verses that I found gave me strength and peace. Again, I wanted to change the future of my own children. Here are some verses that are promises for your children.

"All your children shall be taught by the Lord, and great shall be the peace of your children."

Isaiah 54:13 (NKJV)

"'As for Me,' says the Lord, 'This is My covenant with them; My spirit who is upon you and My Words which I have put in your mouth, shall not depart from your mouth, nor from the mouth of your descendants, nor from your descendants' descendants,' says the Lord, 'from this time and forevermore.'"

Isaiah 59:21 (NKJV)

"The Lord directs the steps of the godly.
He delights in every detail of their lives. Though

they stumble, they will never fall, for the Lord holds them by the hand. The godly always give generous loans to others, and their children are a blessing."

Psalm 37:23-24, 26 (NLT)

"May the Lord give you increase more and more, you and your children. May you be blessed by the Lord, who made heaven and earth."

Psalm 115:14-15 (NKJV)

As I am writing out these verses, I am reminded that change happens as we renew our minds in what the Lord has for us. For example, I had a hard time seeing myself the way that God saw me. I did not change my view until I let the Word dwell in my heart. I love the Lord, and He said that strength and confidence would flood the lovers of God.

"Confidence and strength flood the hearts of the lovers of God who live in awe of Him, and their devotion provides their children with a place of shelter and security."

Proverbs 14:26 (TPT)

Do I always feel strong and confident? No, but the Word says confidence and strength flood the lovers of God. When I do not feel confident or strong, I speak the Word over myself. This is the same thing for speaking over your children or family members. You may not see what you are speaking right away. Do not give up. Keep believing in what God's Word says and keep planting that seed. God wants to restore the broken areas of our lives and make them better than new. What He needs is for us to come into agreement with what He says. When God created, He spoke with Words. We are created in God's image. What we speak, we will create. The problem is complicated because we speak more about the issues than the solutions found in the Word of God. Many of us make our problems bigger than God. Again, I ask you, what are you speaking most? Life or death? It is your choice. I want all that God has for me and my future generations. I have two biological daughters. My heart is not only for my family but for spiritual sons and daughters that I have the privilege to mentor. My prayer lately is, "God make me a strong, healthy, spiritual mom to the future generations." This is what happens when someone finally figures out that the thief has been stealing from them. I am believing for generations, Amen and Amen!

"Now that I am old and gray, don't abandon me, O God. Let me proclaim Your power to this new generation, Your mighty miracles to all who come after me."

Psalm 71:18 (TPT)

"They will tell the world of the lavish splendor of Your kingdom and preach about Your limitless power! They will demonstrate for all to see Your miracles of might and reveal the glorious majesty of Your Kingdom."

Psalm 145:11-12 (TPT)

"Throughout the coming ages we will be the visible display of the infinite, limitless riches of His grace and kindness, which was showered upon us in Jesus Christ."

Ephesians 2:7 (TPT)

Additional Verses about Blessings for the Family

Explore the following verses to build encouragement while you pray over your families.

"But the mercy of the Lord is from everlasting to everlasting on those who fear Him, and His righteousness to children's children, to such as keep His covenant and remember His commandments to do them" (Psalm 103:17-18, NKJV).

"The house of the wicked will be destroyed, but the tent of the godly will flourish" (Proverbs 14:11, NLT).

"As for you because of the blood of my covenant with you, I will free your prisoners from the waterless pit. Return to your fortress, O prisoners of hope; even now I announce that I will restore twice as much to you" (Zechariah 9:11-12 NIV).

"I will give them an undivided heart and put a new spirit in them; I will remove from them their heart of stone and give them a heart of flesh. Then they will follow my decrees and be careful to keep my laws. They will be my people and I will be their God" (Ezekiel 11:19-20, NIV).

"Who then are those that fear the Lord? He will instruct him in the ways they should choose. They will spend their days in prosperity and their descendants will inherit the land. The Lord confides in those who fear Him; He makes His covenant known to them" (Psalm 25:12-14, NIV).

"He will turn the hearts of the fathers to their children and the hearts of the children to their fathers; lest I come and strike the earth with a curse" (Malachi 4:6, NKJV).

"From the Lord comes deliverance: May your blessings be on your people" (Psalm 3:8, NIV).

"He then brought them out and asked, "Sirs, what must I do to be saved? They replied, 'Believe in the Lord Jesus, and you will be saved-you and your household'" (Acts 16:30-31, NIV).

"If anyone observes a fellow believer habitually sinning in a way that doesn't lead to death, you should keep interceding in prayer that God will give that person life" (1 John 5:16a, TPT).

"But From everlasting to everlasting the Lord's love is with those who fear Him, and His righteousness with their children's children—with those who keep His covenant and remember to obey His precept" (Psalm 103:17-18, NIV).

"The Lord opened her heart to respond to Paul's message" (Acts 16:14b, NIV).

"Watch your life and doctrine closely. Persevere in them,

because if you do, you will save both yourself and your hearers" (1 Timothy 4:16, NIV).

"For this is good and acceptable in the sight of God our Savior, who desires all men to be saved and to come to the knowledge of the truth. For there is one God and one mediator between God and man, the man Jesus Christ" (1 Timothy 2:3-5, NKJV).

"And He opened their understanding, that they might comprehend the scriptures" (Luke 24:45, NKJV).

"Jesus answered and said to him, 'If anyone loves me, he will keep My Word, and my Father will love him and We will come to him and make Our home with him. He who does not love Me does not keep my Words; and the Word which you hear is not Mine but the Father's who sent Me'" (John 14:23-24, NKJV).

"Remember me, O Lord, with the favor You have toward your people. Oh visit me with your salvation, that I may see the benefits of your chosen ones, that I may rejoice in the gladness of Your nation, that I may glory with Your inheritance" (Psalm 106:4-5, NKJV).

"I will pour out My Spirit on your descendants and My blessings on your offspring" (Isaiah 44:3b, NKJV).

"Confidence and strength flood the hearts of the lovers of God who live in awe of Him, and their devotion provides their children with a place of shelter and security" (Proverbs 14:26, TPT).

Conclusion

Thank you so much for taking this journey with me through the Word of God. I hope that you clearly see the promises that are available to you as a child of God. They are bought and paid for by the blood of Jesus. God has given each and every one of us a gift through His Son. It is up to each person to choose whether they will open up this gift and receive it. I often look at the life of Jesus. How did He heal the sick? How did He treat people? I have never read any place in the Bible that Jesus pushed Himself on anyone. He just lived and moved through His earthly life looking for relationships, and those who received Him walked away with the healing or blessing. Those who were offended, He let them go on their own way, and He continued on His journey. God will never force Himself on anyone. I hope that through the promises that you can see how much God truly loves you. No matter what you have done or how far you have wandered away from God, He wants to be in a relationship with you. He wants to show you how He sees you. The more you get to know God through His Word, the more you will see the treasures that have been stored up for you. This is just the beginning. There is much more to explore.

The promises have not only given me hope in my day to day journey through life, but they have changed how I see myself. God sees you so much bigger than you see yourself. He has put gifts and talents in each person. As I stated in earlier chapters, I did not think I had what it took to be used by God. I never saw myself as someone able to write a book. I struggled with fear, intimidation, and I felt very inadequate. Here is one of my favorite verses that helped to change that:

> Your anointing has made me strong and mighty. You've empowered my life for triumph by pouring fresh oil over me. Yes! Look how you've made all Your lovers to flourish like palm trees, each one growing in victory, standing with strength! You've transplanted them into Your heavenly courtyard, where they are thriving before You. For in Your presence they will still overflow and be anointed. Even in their old age they will stay fresh, bearing luscious fruit and abiding faithfully. Listen to them! With pleasure they still proclaim: You're so good! You're my beautiful strength! You've never made a mistake with me.

> **Psalm 92:10, 12-15 (TPT)**

I laugh sometimes and tell God that I am so sorry that I took so long to see how He sees me. Thank goodness God never gives up on us. I would remind God of Philippians 1:6 (NKJV):

> "Being confident of this very thing, that He who has begun a good work in you will complete it until the day of Christ Jesus."

I would say, "God, you started this! Your Word says that You will complete what you started in me." I am so grateful for the love of God and His Word. I would not be sharing this book if it weren't for Him. Not too long ago, I heard in my spirit, "Tammy, I did not give you all these verses for you to keep them for yourself!" I knew that I needed to pass along this treasure of promises to give hope to others. Thank goodness for God using friends and family that pushed me out of my comfort zone. I finally had to step out and believe in what God had deposited inside of me. I hope that this book has encouraged you to see things differently. I used a lot of Bible verses so that you could use this as a reference guide for your own journey. I hope that you have enjoyed this adventure in discovering the promises of God. The beauty is that they belong to you. Open the gift that God has given you that has been sitting on the shelf. There is more to discover about God if you will just keep getting to know Him through His Word. Just like a loving parent wanting to bless their children, your Father in heaven wants to do the same for you. I will leave you with this challenge that God gave me.

He said, "Tammy, I will give you what you can believe Me for!" I have been a student in His Word for the past twenty-five years and God has faithfully showed me His promises. It took time to renew, grow, and be stretched, but it was well worth the journey. I have more promises and more to share in future books. I look forward to going on another adventure with you soon. Until then, keep renewing your mind in what God says in His Word and watch Him amaze you!